Stomp to the Rhythm

Teachers' Book

INCLUSIVE READERS SERIES

Stomp to the Rhythm

Teachers' Book

Maggie Walker
Val Davis
Ann Berger

David Fulton Publishers
London

David Fulton Publishers Ltd
Ormond House
26–27 Boswell Street
London WC1N 3JZ

First published in Great Britain in 2002 by David Fulton Publishers Ltd

Copyright © 2002 Maggie Walker, Val Davis, Ann Berger
Illustrations © 2002 Suzi Woollatt of Graham-Cameron Illustration
Writing with Symbols © 2002 Widgit Software

British Library Cataloguing in Publication Data
A catalogue record is available from the British Library.

ISBN: 1-85346-890-8

The materials in this publication may be photocopied only for use within the purchasing organisation. Otherwise, all rights reserved. No part of this publication may be reproduced, stored in a retrieval system or transmitted in any form or by any means, electronic, mechanical, photocopying, recording or otherwise, without the prior permission of the publisher.

Acknowledgements:
The publishers would like to thank Tony Mitton for permission to include his poems:
'Make a Face', from *Unzip Your Lips Again*, published by Macmillan, 1999; and 'Arabian Nights', from *First Verses*, published by Oxford University Press, 1996.

Designed and typeset by Kenneth Burnley, Wirral, Cheshire.
Illustrations on pages 45, 46, 48 by Caroline Burnley.
Printed and bound in Great Britain by Bell and Bain Ltd, Glasgow.

Contents

Introduction	vii
Weekly plan for each level from P1–2C	1
Suggestions for further activities	4
List of items for a multisensory pack	6
Symbols	7
Word strips	9

Two differentiated versions of the text with symbols for pupils working at:
    levels P5–P6
    levels P7–1C

Differentiated version of the text for pupils working at levels 1B–2C

Ten examples of resource sheets for use with the suggested activities:

Resource Sheet 1: Rhyming words	43
Resource Sheet 2: Draw a face	44
Resource Sheet 3: Which part of the body?	45
Resource Sheet 4: Make a wish	46
Resource Sheet 5: Monkey tricks	47
Resource Sheet 6: Dreams	48
Resource Sheet 7: Plurals	49
Resource Sheet 8: Peanut butter and jelly	50
Resource Sheet 9: 'ing' words	51
Resource Sheet 10: Fireworks	52

Note: All of these resources may be photocopied, cut out and laminated as required.

Introduction

Pupils who are at the early stages of acquiring literacy skills need motivating texts to support their learning. The Inclusive Readers series of books is designed to provide this. It is based on the scheme of work developed by Bristol Schools, which has been published in the second edition of *Implementing the Literacy Hour for Pupils with Learning Difficulties* (David Fulton 2001).

The big books include fiction, non-fiction styles and poetry, and each individual book focuses on one specific genre that should be covered in Key Stage 2. Some of the texts are also suitable for use with pupils in Years 7 and 8. In the centre of each big book is a pull-out section, which features characters and objects from the texts that can be cut out and laminated, and used to support multisensory teaching strategies. Each Teachers' Book includes a wide range of activities that can be used with pupils to reinforce their understanding of the text and the development of word and sentence level skills. They are linked to the Key Stage 1 objectives in the national Literacy Strategy but designed to be appropriate for pupils between 7 and 12 years of age.

The Teachers' Book also includes three differentiated texts based on the big book, which are designed to be used during guided reading work. They are produced at three levels linked to the revised P scales. The P5–P6 and P7–1C books have symbols as well as words to reinforce reading skills. The level 1B–2C books have only words. Each of these differentiated texts is illustrated with black and white versions of the pictures from the big book, and is fully photocopiable for individual use, and also for parents to support pupils at home.

We have worked closely with Widgit Software to develop appropriate symbols for certain key words. These symbols can be copied and used in other contexts to reinforce the learning. They are also available for words with symbols.

The poems in this big book collection were almost all chosen for their strong rhythm and rhyme. All the poems can be accompanied by different actions by the children in class or in drama. They cover a range of ideas and movements from the stealth of 'The Gecko' to the stomp of 'Pulsation'.

National Literacy Strategy

Weekly Plan

Class _____ Teacher _____ Date _____

	Whole class shared reading and writing	Whole class phonics, spelling, vocabulary and grammar	Guided group tasks P1–P2	Guided group tasks P3–P4	Plenary
Mon	STOMP TO THE RHYTHM UNITED TOGETHER	Pupils indicate (actively or coactively) each part of their bodies as they are mentioned in the poem	Use a variety of materials, e.g. feathers, sandpaper, silk, to raise awareness of parts of the pupils' own bodies	Pupils make hand, feet, finger, elbow and /or knee prints	How aware are pupils of their own bodies? Can they indicate parts of their own bodies?
Tues		Use a doll or a puppet for pupils to indicate body parts	Make a photograph book of each pupil's face. Can they recognise: themselves? other pupils?	Use body prints (see above) to play a matching game	Which parts of their own (or puppet's) body can pupils identify?
Wed		Make a collection of shoes and gloves and try them all on	Manipulate some play dough or clay. Emphasise the use of hands or feet	What can you do with your hands? Clap. What can you do with your eyes? Blink. Your lips? Kiss, etc.	How are pupils responding to the poem?
Thur		Look at pictures of facial expressions, e.g. laughing, crying, surprised, afraid	Play some hand/feet games. For younger pupils – this little piggy; round and round the garden. For older pupils – stone, paper, scissors; cheesy feet	Try putting together some simple body part jigsaws or make a big cardboard body (draw around one pupil?) and cut in into pieces before putting it back together again	How do pupils respond to facial expressions?
Fri	Adult reads poem and pauses at some of the body parts for pupils' anticipation		Look at some pictures of body parts, e.g. LDA cards or jigsaw puzzle pieces	Look at the symbols for some body parts. Can pupils indicate which body part is identified?	Which pictures or symbols of body parts can pupils 'read'?

National Literacy Strategy

Weekly Plan

Class _____ Teacher _____ Date _____

	Whole class shared reading and writing	**Whole class phonics, spelling, vocabulary and grammar**	**Guided group tasks P5–P6**	**Guided group tasks P7–P8**	**Plenary**
Mon	STOMP TO THE RHYTHM MAKE A FACE	Adults and pupils make each face described in the poem. Have a competition to find the ugliest	Pupils draw a face suggested by the poem. A friend makes the face he has drawn	Draw a face and write a caption	Assess drawing and writing skills by looking at some pupils' work together
Tues		Think of words that rhyme with 'face'. Make a list together	Make paper plate faces	Match pairs of words from the poem and read them to each other	Which words can pupils read?
Wed	Adult writes on a board or paper as many words as pupils can remember which describe the faces		Trace over some of the words in the poem, e.g. fat, dog, cat, thin, mad. Try copying them underneath	Write phrases and sentences using the words on the board from the whole group activity	Which words and letters can pupils write?
Thur	Talk about words which go together, e.g. sweet as honey, sharp, snarl and snappy. Make up some to go with other words, e.g. fat, mad, true		Make a collage of faces cut from magazines	Pupils write the word 'ace' several times down the page. Then add letters to the beginning of each and read what they have written	Are pupils beginning to understand about using adjectives?
Fri		Talk about how important faces are in understanding others	Match pairs of CVC words from the poem, e.g. mad, fat, sad	Make simple phrases from single word strips, e.g. sad face, happy face, mad face. Read them to each other	What are the pupils' opinions of the poem?

National Literacy Strategy

Weekly Plan

Class _____ Teacher _____ Date _____

	Whole class shared reading and writing	**Whole class phonics, spelling, vocabulary and grammar**	**Guided group tasks 1C–1A**	**Guided group tasks 2C–2A**	**Plenary**
Mon	STOMP TO THE RHYTHM ARABIAN NIGHT	Talk about magic, genie's, flying carpets, wishes etc.	Illustrate a photocopy of the poem	Illustrate a photocopy of the poem	How many words from the poem can pupils already read?
Tues		Pass a 'magic' ring around. Make a wish	Draw what your wish would be if you found the ring and write a sentence about it	Write what your wish would be if you found the ring	Let pupils vote which is the best wish
Wed		Put a plasticene figure in a bottle. Whisper a favour to it	Draw a genie. Write what he/she might say to you	Write a spell for a genie to say	Ask a few pupils to read their own writing to the class
Thur		Sit together on a 'magic' carpet and imagine a story	Draw a picture of the magic carpet flying over a special place. Write a caption	Imagine that you saw a flying carpet. Describe what it would be like	How imaginative are the pupils?
Fri		Talk about whether you would prefer the magic ring, the genie or the flying carpet and why	Find all the words in the poem which rhyme	Write a magic story of your own	See if anyone can read the poem all the way through

National Literacy Strategy

Suggestions for further activities

Text: *Stomp to the Rhythm*

P1–P2
- Clap, stamp, tap, beat the rhythms of the poems
- Use a monkey puppet to make the actions in 'Monkey Tricks'
- Use sparklers and candles in a darkened room to create the atmosphere for 'Firework'
- Look at flames made by candles (Firework)
- Track patterns made by sparklers (Firework)
- Make a book about things you like, perhaps with photographs (My Robot)
- Taste peanut butter and jelly (Peanut Butter and Jelly)

P3–P4
- Make firework pictures using fluorescent paints or wax resist (Firework)
- Make a tape of sounds to play to others in the group (Pulsation)
- Colour (scribble over) a picture of a monkey (Monkey Tricks)
- Taste peanut butter, stick it to the roof of your mouth and try getting it off in ways suggested by 'Peanut Butter'
- Try to make all the sounds in 'Pulsation'
- Squash and squeeze peanut butter and jelly for 'Peanut Butter and Jelly'
- Make peanut butter and jelly sandwiches to taste for 'Peanut Butter and Jelly'
- Draw yourself (United Together)
- Make body music. Copy rhythms suggested by an adult or other pupils (Pulsation)

P5–P6
- Make a scribble firework picture (Firework)
- Draw lots of magic rings. Make each one a different colour (Arabian Night)
- Make up a dance for 'Dream Variation'
- Read two of the poems and decide which one you like best
- Find all the words in this poem beginning with . . .

- Fold a piece of paper in half. Make one half a day picture and the other half a night picture (Dream Variation)
- Using word strips reading 'one' and 'two', match them to pictures of legs, arms, ears, head, heart and so on (United Together)
- Using photocopied faces with no features, make as many expressions as you can (Make a Face)

P7–P8

- Write about what else monkeys do (Monkey Tricks)
- Add labels e.g. legs, arms, nose to a picture of a body (United Together)
- Find all the words in the book which begin with the same letter as your name
- Talk about dreams for 'Dream Variation'.
- Mime all the actions in 'My Robot'
- Move along like a gecko. Then try moving like other creatures (Gecko)
- Find all the three letter words with 'a' as the medial vowel in 'Make a Face'. Read them to a friend. Can you think of any more?
- Make a flick book showing the gecko's tongue catching flies (Gecko)

1C–1B

- Write or draw what would you ask your robot to do for you (My Robot)
- Write down the two words that end with 'ing' and then think of some more 'ing' words (Gecko)
- Write as many words as you can which describe fireworks (Firework)
- Draw a picture of a genie and write what he/she might say in a speech bubble (Arabian Night)
- Carefully copy a few lines from the poem you like best

1A–2C

- Discuss the 'the human race' and what makes us the same yet different (United Together)
- Write some words which describe fireworks (Fireworks)
- Write the recipe for your favourite sandwich (Peanut Butter and Jelly)
- Write all the letters of the alphabet down a piece of paper. Write one word for each letter from the book
- Write another word which means the same as . . . Use a dictionary to help (Gecko)
- Talk about the difference between poems and stories

Multisensory pack

United Together
Dolls

Monkey Tricks
Monkey puppets

Gecko
Photocopy of gecko picture. Stick small pieces of velcro on each toe

Firework
Sparklers
Candles

Arabian Night
Silver dish
Ring
Glass bottle (flask shaped)
Carpet sample

My Robot
Robot toy

Peanut Butter and Jelly
Peanut butter
Jelly
Peanuts in their shells
Bread
Butter

Pulsation
Wooden stick
Washboard or similar
Brass bell or cup
Glass
Sand in a tin
Saucepan lids
Beaters

Symbols

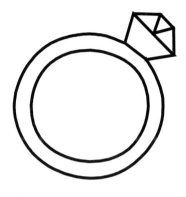

ring

wish

genie

carpet

fly

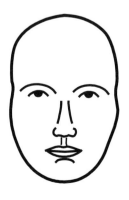

face

mad

sad

funny

happy

snappy

Word strips

List 1

I	can
a	this
is	my
in	you
the	and
it	look
at	see

Word strips

List 2

here	make
first	take
then	what
your	

Word strips

Context words

ring	wish
genie	carpet
fly	fat
face	thin
mad	sad
funny	happy
snappy	bread
bake	peanut(s)
butter	jelly
knife	cut
crack	mash
spread	smear
sandwich	eat
feel	wobbling
belly	

Differentiated versions of the text

On the following pages you will find three differentiated versions of the story *Stomp to the Rhythm*, for use with individual pupils working at the following levels:

The version for pupils working at levels P5–6 uses the following key words:

HF words List 1	is a away
List 2	here make
Context words	ring wish genie carpet fly

The version for pupils working at levels P7–1C uses the following key words:

HF words List 1	I can a look at my you see this is
List 2	make what your
Context words	fat face thin mad sad funny happy snappy

The version for pupils working at levels 1B–2C uses the following key words:

HF words List 1	you the and it a I can in my
List 2	first take then them
Context words	bread bake peanut(s) butter jelly knife cut crack mash spread smear sandwich eat feel wobbling belly

Each of these texts can be photocopied and made into individual books. We have also included a black and white version of the cover of the story book which can be copied, laminated and used for individual book covers.

Stomp to the Rhythm

Chosen by Maggie Walker

Illustrated by Suzi Woollatt

Text for pupils working at levels P5–P6

Here is a ring.

Make a wish.

Make a wish.

Here is a genie.

Make a wish.

Make a wish.

Here is a carpet.

Fly away!

Stomp to the Rhythm

Chosen by Maggie Walker

Illustrated by Suzi Woollatt

Text for pupils working at levels P7–1C

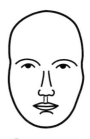

I can make a fat face.

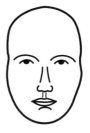

Look at my fat face.

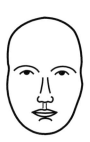

I can make a thin face.

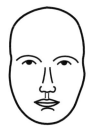

Look at my thin face.

I can make a mad face.

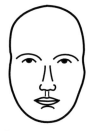

Can you make a mad face?

I can make a sad face.

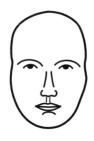

Can you make a sad face?

I can make a funny face.

What funny face can you make?

I can make a happy face.

What happy face can you make?

I can make a snappy face.

Can you see my snappy face?

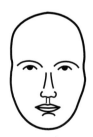

This face is my face.

Can you see your face?

Stomp to the Rhythm

Chosen by Maggie Walker

Illustrated by Suzi Woollatt

Text for pupils working at levels 1B–2C

First you take the bread and bake it, bake it.
Peanut butter, peanut butter, jelly, jelly.

Then you take a knife and cut it, cut it.
Peanut butter, peanut butter, jelly, jelly.

Then you take the peanuts and crack them, crack them.
Peanut butter, peanut butter, jelly, jelly.

Then you take the peanuts and mash them, mash them.
Peanut butter, peanut butter, jelly, jelly.

Then you take a knife and spread it, spread it.
Peanut butter, peanut butter, jelly, jelly.

Then you take the jelly and smear it, smear it.
Peanut butter, peanut butter, jelly, jelly.

Then you take the sandwich and eat it, eat it.
Peanut butter, peanut butter, jelly, jelly.

Peanut butter, peanut butter, jelly, jelly.
I can feel it wobbling in my belly.

Rhyming words

RESOURCE SHEET 1

Name _____

Match the rhyming words:

toes	hold
trees	nose
bike	head
beat	like
gold	knees
bed	dishes
fishes	heat

Draw a face

RESOURCE SHEET 2

Name _____

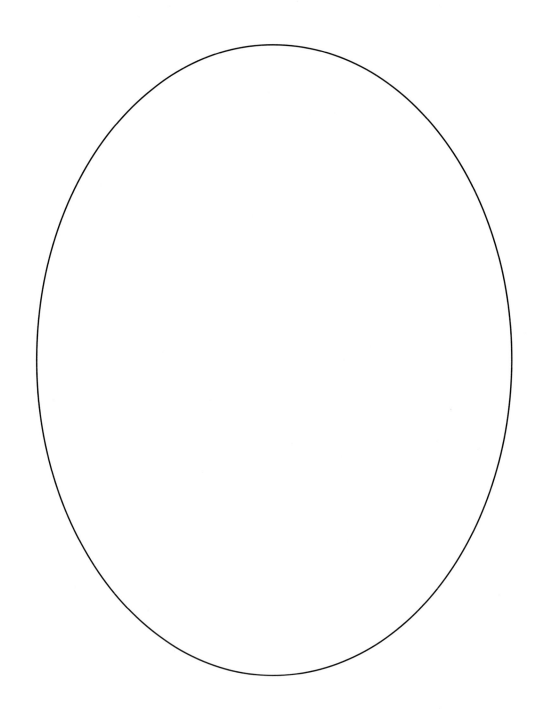

Which part of the body?

RESOURCE SHEET 3

Name _____

Cut out the words and stick them on the correct part of the picture:

| head | foot | arm | leg | hand |

45

Make a wish

<u>RESOURCE SHEET 4</u>

Name _____

What would you wish for? Colour the genie and write your wish next to him.

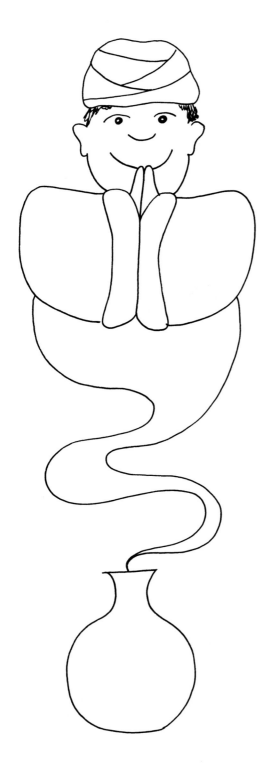

Monkey tricks

RESOURCE SHEET 5

Name _____

Copy and colour in the Mighty Monkey.

Dreams

RESOURCE SHEET 6

Name _____

What do you dream about? Draw or write your dreams here.

Plurals

RESOURCE SHEET 7

Name _____

Make all these words plural:

leg	
arm	
eye	
finger	
toe	
face	
nose	
lip	
ear	

Peanut butter and jelly

RESOURCE SHEET 8

Name _____

This is a recipe for peanut butter and jelly sandwiches. Copy the sentences but put them in the correct order:

Put peanut butter on the butter

Eat the sandwich

Put jelly on the peanut butter

Put butter on the bread

Fold the bread

'ing' words

RESOURCE SHEET 9

Name _____

Make all these words 'ing' words. Read them to your teacher or a friend:

play	
eat	
sing	
read	
drink	
jump	
run	
write	
dance	

Fireworks

RESOURCE SHEET 10

Name _____

Draw a firework that makes the sound of the word:

Whizz

Bang

Wheeeeeee

Fizzzzzzz

Whoosh

Shhhhhhhh